"*Step 4* is raw, unfiltered, and honest. Brandon Couch doesn't write from a place of theory or safe distance; he writes from the trenches of addiction, loss, shame, and grace. His story is a lifeline for anyone who has ever felt too far gone, too broken, or too ashamed to speak up. What you'll find here isn't perfection—it's progress, hope, and the reminder that healing is messy but possible. Brandon reminds us all that light really does shine through the darkness."

—**Rev. Ryan Canaday,**
Founder, Pastor & Executive Director of
FREE Recovery Community
in Denver, Colorado

"These pages tell a story of beauty from ashes, strength from passivity, and love from hate. It's a good, good story. Stories like these, when shared, breathe hope into those still trapped behind bars—and into those who love them and long for more. Hope is a dangerous thing. And I know Brandon is committed to offering it to anyone willing to honor his journey with the turn of another page.

I love what Brandon writes in the later pages of *Step 4: My life became a mirror, a ministry, a mission.* I hope that for my life too."

—**Michael Thompson,**
Author of *The Heart of a Warrior*

STEP 4

A JOURNEY THROUGH ADDICTION

BRANDON COUCH

LUCIDBOOKS

Step 4: A Journey Through Addiction

Copyright © 2025 by Brandon Couch

Published by Lucid Books, Houston, TX
www.LucidBooks.com

All rights reserved. No part of this publication may be reproduced, stored in a retrieval system, or transmitted in any form by any means, electronic, mechanical, photocopy, recording, or otherwise, without the prior permission of the publisher, except as provided for by US copyright laws.

Unless otherwise indicated, scripture quotations are taken from the Holy Bible, New International Version®, NIV®. Copyright ©1973, 1978, 1984, 2011 by Biblica, Inc.™ Used by permission of Zondervan. All rights reserved worldwide. www.zondervan.com The "NIV" and "New International Version" are trademarks registered in the United States Patent and Trademark Office by Biblica, Inc.™

Scripture quotations marked (MSG) are taken from THE MESSAGE, copyright © 1993, 2002, 2018 by Eugene H. Peterson. Used by permission of NavPress. All rights reserved. Represented by Tyndale House Publishers, Inc.

ISBN: 978-1-63296-835-7
eISBN: 978-1-63296-836-4

Special Sales: Most Lucid Books titles are available in special quantity discounts. Custom imprinting or excerpting can also be done to fit special needs. Contact Lucid Books at Info@LucidBooks.com.

*To my son and daughter.
You are my why.
In the wreckage, in the rebuild,
in my fight to be a better father,
I carry you.
You didn't ask for this story,
but I pray it shows you the strength in scars
and the beauty in becoming.*

*To the ones still lost in the dark,
I know that place.
This is a light I lit for you.
Follow it home.*

*To those who stood beside me
when I had nothing to offer,
your love stitched me back together.*

*And to the God who never walked away,
this story is Yours.
All of it.*

CONTENTS

Preface xi

Introduction: The Strength Within 1

Chapter 1: Losing My Way 5

Chapter 2: Addiction and Adultery 9

Chapter 3: Seeking God – A Desperate Attempt 13

Chapter 4: Where I Left Off 17

Chapter 5: Back to Cincinnati 19

Chapter 6: Juggling Masks 25

Chapter 7: First Big Scare 29

Chapter 8: Employment Problems and Car Crashes 33

Chapter 9: Mom's Passing 39

Chapter 10: An Honest Attempt at Sobriety 45

Chapter 11: A New Low 49

Chapter 12: Depression 55

Chapter 13: New Home 59

Chapter 14: Losing More 63

Chapter 15: Another Attempt at Rehab 67

Chapter 16: Lonely 73

Chapter 17: Crystal Meth 77

Chapter 18: Jail and Prison 81

Chapter 19: Learning to Stay..85

Chapter 20: Surrender..87

Chapter 21: The Birth of the Recovery Couch...................91

Chapter 22: Fruit of the Couch 95

Chapter 23: Full Circle..99

Epilogue 103

A Note to My Children 105

Next Steps and Resources 107

SPECIAL THANKS

To my family—thank you for loving me through the worst and believing in who I could become. Your prayers, your patience, and your presence kept me anchored when I had nothing left.

To my mentors, counselors, and spiritual leaders—thank you for speaking truth, even when it hurt. Your wisdom and accountability helped shape this journey and kept me moving forward.

To my friends in recovery—your honesty, your stories, and your willingness to show up raw and real reminded me I wasn't alone. You taught me how to keep fighting one day at a time.

To Lucid Books—thank you for seeing the value in my story and helping me bring it to life with excellence and integrity. Megan, your first call felt like a divine appointment. Thank you for your honesty, encouragement, and belief in what this book could become.

And to the readers—thank you for picking up this book. I pray something on these pages speaks directly to your soul.

Above all, thank You, God, for grace that never ran out and mercy that met me right in the mess.

PREFACE

This book wasn't written from a mountaintop. It was written from the valley.

Step 4 began as a journal entry—a personal inventory, a desperate attempt to make sense of the chaos I created and the pain I caused. I never imagined it would become something others would read, let alone something that might help someone else heal.

But God has a way of using broken pieces. He takes what we try to hide and in His mercy turns it into something useful—even beautiful. This story is not told from a place of perfection but from a place of progress. It's not clean or polished. It's real. It's messy. It's honest.

I didn't write this to impress you. I wrote it to reach you.

If you're holding this book, I believe there's a reason. Maybe you're in the fight of your life. Maybe you love someone who is. Or maybe you're just tired of pretending you're okay.

Wherever you are, welcome.

This is the journey I took through addiction, shame, grace, and healing.

And if it helps you take your next step—even one—then every word is worth it.

INTRODUCTION
THE STRENGTH WITHIN

Life isn't easy. It never has been. It will test you, push you, and try to break you. It will throw obstacles in your path when you least expect them. Just when you think you're standing tall, life has a way of knocking you back down, daring you to rise again. I know this because I've lived it. I've felt the weight of failure, the sting of rejection, and the emptiness of loss. But if there's one thing I've learned it's that toughness isn't about avoiding hardship; it's about facing it head on.

Looking back, I can pinpoint the exact moments that shaped me, the trials that forged my resilience like fire hardens steel. There were times I wanted to quit, times when giving up seemed like the easier path. But something inside me, something deeper than pain or fear, wouldn't let me. That something was toughness.

Toughness isn't just about physical strength. It's mental. It's emotional. It's spiritual. It's the ability to keep going when every part of you wants to stop. It's waking up when exhaustion begs you to stay in bed. It's pushing forward when fear tells you to turn back. It's believing in yourself when no one else does.

When I think about the people I admire—the champions, the leaders, the survivors—I don't see people who had it easy. I see people who faced failure, who endured loss, who stood at the edge of defeat and still found a way to fight back. That's real toughness. That's what I wanted to become.

Toughness is built in the moments when no one is watching. It's built in the dark hours of struggle, in the sacrifices you make for a dream no one else can see but you. And the truth is, nothing worth having comes easily. Nothing great is built without struggle.

I didn't always understand this. There was a time when I thought life was supposed to be fair and that success was a straight path. But I learned that growth comes through adversity. The moments that nearly broke me were the moments that made me. I had to embrace the challenges, see the setbacks as stepping stones, and use the pain as fuel.

If you're reading this, you might be facing your own battles. You might be questioning your strength, wondering if you have what it takes to make it through. Let me tell you this: You are stronger than you know. You are more powerful than you realize. And if you refuse to quit, if you refuse to let life defeat you, then nothing—nothing—can stop you.

This is my story. It's not just about the struggles but about the lessons, the triumphs, and the moments of clarity that came from surviving the storm. It's about learning that tough times don't last, but tough people do. And in the end, toughness isn't just about surviving; it's about thriving.

So let's begin.

CHAPTER 1

LOSING MY WAY

While I was on active duty in the United States Air Force, I moved with my wife at the time to Ellsworth Air Force Base in Rapid City, South Dakota. This move marked the beginning of our new life as husband and wife. We were both excited and nervous about this fresh start, leaving behind everything familiar in Cincinnati, Ohio, for a place 18 hours away.

We shared a passion for physical fitness and recreational softball. During that first summer in South Dakota, we made many friends as we played coed softball and traveled to tournaments in the area. Life felt good, full of camaraderie and adventure. We were young, active, and building a future together.

As our second winter in South Dakota approached, we decided it was time to start a family. It didn't take long before we received the greatest news of our lives—my wife was pregnant. We were overjoyed, imagining our future as parents to our baby boy, later named Aiden. Life felt like it was falling into place. We were building something special, something that mattered.

And then everything changed.

Shortly after celebrating the good news, my life took a drastic turn. During a mandatory Air Force physical training session, I suffered an injury that would alter the course of my life. About halfway into a 5 km run, I suddenly lost all feeling in my left leg.

I had always taken immense pride in my physical fitness. The idea of quitting was unthinkable, especially in the Air Force where going on a waiver was seen as a sign of weakness. So with no feeling in my leg, I pushed through, forcing myself to finish the run. Even now, it remains the strangest and scariest physical ailment I have ever experienced.

After the run, I reported to work as usual, hoping the feeling in my leg would return. But the pain only intensified. Sharp, shooting pain and numbness in my left leg made even the simplest tasks unbearable. After struggling through half a day in extreme discomfort, I finally went to the base hospital where the doctors immediately began running a series of tests to assess the damage.

For weeks, they examined my range of motion, performed imaging tests, and tried to determine the extent of my injury. Finally, the diagnosis came, and it was worse than I could have imagined. The doctor looked me in the eyes and listed the damages: sciatica, ruptured discs, disc herniations, and torn thecal sacs in my lower lumbar.

I remember swallowing hard and saying, "That sounds bad."

His response was blunt. "It is."

With those words, my life took a sharp turn. The Air Force had shaped me to be strong, to push through pain, to never show weakness. But this injury wasn't something I could just shake off. As I was handed my first prescription—120 pills of 5 mg Vicodin for pain and another 120 pills of 5 mg Valium for muscle spasms. I had no idea that this moment would mark the beginning of my spiral into addiction.

CHAPTER 2

ADDICTION AND ADULTERY

At first, the pills numbed the stress of being an active-duty Airman in the United States Air Force. I welcomed the relief, leaning into it as a crutch rather than a concern. The long hours, the pressure, the weight of duty—all of it seemed easier to bear under the influence of Vicodin and Valium.

But after a year, the prescribed doses no longer had the same effect. My body had adapted, and I needed more to reach the same level of escape. My doctor obliged, increasing my dosage to 10 mg of Vicodin and 10 mg of Valium four times a day—twice the previous amount, twice the dependence.

Deep down, I knew I had a problem. Subconsciously, the signs were there. The funny thing is that I had always believed addiction was just a weakness, a lack of willpower. I was ignorant of how drugs rewired the brain and gripped the body with an unrelenting force. So I brushed off my concerns. After all, I was functioning, wasn't I?

The timing of my growing dependence coincided with my reassignment to Charleston Air Force Base in South Carolina. It was a welcome escape from the brutal winters of South Dakota but also a fresh environment where I'd be forming new relationships.

Each morning in Charleston, I woke with the same unsettling realization—I needed my medication before I could function, before I could even feel like myself. The thought gnawed at me, eroding my sense of control. It wasn't just the pills that changed me. Losing my usual outlets made things worse. Before my injury, I found validation in physical activity—exercise, sports, and the camaraderie that came with both. But the Air Force doesn't allow injured service members to participate in those things, so that source of self-worth was gone.

My wife saw the changes in me. She watched my decline, likely unsure how to confront it. I still remember the day she asked gently but directly if I thought I had a problem with my medication. I reacted the way addicts often do. I got defensive, offended, and angry. I denied it, put on a tough exterior, and convinced myself I was still in control. But inside, I was crumbling.

Looking back, I wish I had been honest with her and with myself. If I had acknowledged my dependence, if I had taken responsibility before I spiraled, I could have spared us both so much pain. But instead, I let my pride morph into something even uglier—arrogance.

Addiction and Adultery

At work, I sought validation in dangerous places. A woman in my unit became a distraction, a temporary salve for the emptiness I felt. It started as harmless flirtation. At least that's how I justified it. But deep down, I knew better. I even confided in a friend, asking him to hold me accountable and help me avoid making a mistake I couldn't undo. But addiction doesn't care about accountability. It thrives in secrecy and self-deception.

If you play with fire long enough, you get burned. And I did.

I did the unthinkable.

I was unfaithful to my wife, my family, and the vows I had made before God.

I had spent so much time trying to numb my pain that I created even more.

CHAPTER 3

SEEKING GOD – A DESPERATE ATTEMPT

My immediate response to my unfaithfulness was to seek God and repent. The guilt and remorse had become unbearable, suffocating me under their weight. I needed relief, a way to cleanse my soul, to somehow make things right.

I had been attending NewSpring Church, and I loved it there. It felt like home, a place where I could be vulnerable, where I could believe in the possibility of redemption. So as the new year approached, I made a resolution. I would go to church every Sunday for an entire year. I convinced myself that if I showed up consistently, if I surrounded myself with worship and Scripture, maybe God would convict me enough to guide me toward healing—toward a way out of the mess I had created.

But as the weeks passed, I came to a sobering realization. I couldn't expect God to fix my problems while I was still hiding from the truth. Repentance wasn't about showing up on Sundays; it was about surrender.

On one Sunday, the pastor invited anyone in need of prayer to seek out a member of the prayer team after the service. The moment the service ended, I didn't hesitate. I needed that prayer. My heart pounded as I made a beeline to the first person I could find. I remember that encounter like it was yesterday.

My hands were clammy as I approached a man with glasses. His expression was open and kind. He introduced himself as Dylan. In my head, I kept repeating, *Be honest. Just be honest.* But when I opened my mouth, the full truth refused to come out.

"I'm struggling," I admitted. "I need prayer about my medication."

But I kept the affair locked inside, buried under layers of fear—fear of judgment, fear of losing my wife, fear of what it would mean to confess it out loud.

Dylan prayed for me, and before I left, we exchanged phone numbers. I had no idea at the time that he would become an incredible resource, a lifeline when I needed one most. Over the next several weeks, we met occasionally for coffee. Our conversations centered on my dependence on medication, how I was coping, and where I was spiritually.

But one day, I couldn't hold it in any longer. The affair was eating me alive. The weight of it—the shame, the deception—was unbearable. It had festered for too long, and I finally broke. I told Dylan everything.

His response wasn't what I expected. He didn't judge me

or offer easy answers. Instead, he showed humility and honesty. He admitted that he didn't know how to handle it. And that made me respect him even more.

"Let me seek wisdom from others," he said, "and I'll get back to you."

I agreed, hoping—praying—that a solution to my agony was near.

A few days later, Dylan got back to me. He said we should meet with a man named Brenden at the church office in Charleston. Again, I agreed, desperate for any direction, any glimmer of a way forward.

In that meeting, Brenden gave me the advice I didn't want but needed to hear.

"You have to be honest with your wife," he said.

Looking back, I know it was the right advice. But in that moment, it felt impossible.

I left the meeting with a 20-minute drive ahead of me, my mind racing. As I turned on the car radio, a song filled the silence— "When a Woman's Fed Up" by R. Kelly.

The lyrics pierced straight through me.

Tears blurred my vision.

I wept uncontrollably.

Instead of driving home, I circled the block again and again, stretching the 20-minute drive to 45. I wasn't ready. I knew what I had to do, but I was terrified.

God was summoning me to be honest—to confess, to face the consequences of my actions.

And yet I kept driving.

CHAPTER 4

WHERE I LEFT OFF

I couldn't bear the thought of losing my wife. So I ignored the advice I had been given to confess the affair. Instead, I buried the truth beneath a growing pile of lies and numbed my emotions with Vicodin and Valium. The more I avoided reality, the more distance I created between me and my wife.

Rather than face my shame, I sought distraction. I spent countless nights glued to my tablet, binge-watching Netflix until the early hours of the morning. Looking back, I see it clearly. I was desperately searching for any way to escape the truth.

But even my escape had its limits.

The pills that once provided relief were losing their potency. My body had adjusted, demanding more to achieve the same numbing effect. So I added NyQuil to my nightly routine, hoping it would help me sleep. At this point, I was taking 10 mg of Vicodin four times a day, 10 mg of Valium four times a day, and washing it all down with a swig of NyQuil at bedtime.

My body was fighting back. Night after night, I woke up drenched in sweat. The toxins were seeping from my pores, leaving behind an odor so distinct, so unnatural, that even now I can still remember it. My body was trying to warn me, trying to purge what I was poisoning it with. But in active addiction, I didn't care about warning signs.

Then came more bad news. As my time in Charleston was coming to an end, I received word from the medical team. The Air Force was medically retiring me due to the structural damage in my back. My career—my identity—was slipping away, and yet my biggest concern wasn't my future. It was my next dose.

The drugs were wearing off more quickly. The feeling I once relied on was fading faster and faster. It terrified me.

Then came another complication. The medication had suppressed my breathing so much that fluid had built up in my lungs, leading to a diagnosis of pneumonia. When my doctor prescribed a codeine-based cough syrup, I didn't see it as a warning sign. I saw it as another opportunity, another high.

Now I was taking 10 mg of Vicodin four times a day, 10 mg of Valium four times a day, and multiple doses of codeine cough syrup. My addiction had escalated beyond anything I had ever imagined. And yet I felt nothing.

My marriage was falling apart. I was drowning in addiction. I was about to be unemployed. But as long as I was high, none of it seemed to matter.

CHAPTER 5

BACK TO CINCINNATI

When my time in Charleston came to an end, my unit threw me a going-away party at a local restaurant. At the end of the luncheon, I stood up to thank everyone, making my way around the room and offering personalized words of appreciation. But when I got to my wife and son, a wave of emotion hit me like a tidal wave.

In front of everyone, I wept uncontrollably.

Our chapter in the United States Air Force had officially closed. The life we had built was packed into boxes, and we were heading back to Cincinnati, Ohio. At the time, I still didn't recognize my addiction for what it was. I had no prescribing doctor anymore and was instructed to seek medical care through the Cincinnati Veterans Affairs (VA).

At my first visit to the VA, I was told I needed to register as a patient before receiving treatment.

"How long will that take?" I asked.

"A couple of months," they responded.

Unaware that my body had developed a full-blown dependence on Vicodin and Valium, I accepted the wait without much concern. I had no idea that within days I would experience my first round of withdrawal.

Withdrawal and Denial

My first day without my medication coincided with the arrival of our household goods in Cincinnati. As movers carried in furniture and boxes, I tried to organize things but felt increasingly weak. My energy was nonexistent, and every movement felt like a monumental effort. I thought I was coming down with the flu.

I kept sneaking off to sit down, pretending to take a break but really just trying to conserve what little energy I had. Eventually, I started hiding from the movers, isolating myself to rest.

Now I recognize that feeling all too well—the aching bones, the relentless fatigue, the cold sweats. But back then, I was still blind to my addiction. I had no idea that this was just the beginning.

Meanwhile, my wife was spending most of her time either at work or sleeping at her parents' house. She was torn, wrestling with the painful choice between staying in the chaos I had created or freeing herself from it.

Every time she edged closer to leaving, I latched onto an opportunity that made it seem like things were finally turning around.

A Temporary Fix

The first of these opportunities came when I was hired at the Veterans Resource Station at Northern Kentucky University (NKU). Around the same time, I was finally registered at the Cincinnati VA and assigned a physician. When I met with my new doctor, I insisted on being put back on my medications, despite her hesitations.

With my prescriptions refilled, I convinced myself that I was ready to reenter the workforce. I also applied to NKU's Physical Education Bachelor's program and was accepted. My Montgomery Post-9/11 GI Bill benefits meant I would receive a housing allowance while attending school, along with part-time income from my job.

With a structured plan in place, my wife started staying at home more often. Looking back, I realize she was rooting for me the whole time. I just couldn't see it then.

Addiction Tightens Its Grip

At the Veterans Resource Station, my job was to help fellow veterans navigate their education benefits. For many, this was a life-changing opportunity, one that I, too, should have been grateful for. But after just two semesters, I was in a rapid downward spiral once again.

My top priority was no longer school or work. It was my medication.

I began abusing my prescriptions and simultaneously

smoking massive amounts of marijuana. On weekends, I threw alcohol into the mix. My decision-making deteriorated, and once again, my wife had one foot out the door.

My prescribing doctor noticed the warning signs and began requiring drug tests at my monthly checkups. She made it clear that if I tested positive for anything I wasn't prescribed, she would stop writing my Vicodin prescriptions. However, my Valium was now being prescribed by a psychiatrist at the Clermont County VA, who never required drug tests.

To keep smoking weed while still passing my urine screenings, I bought a Whizzinator, a fake male appendage designed to hold clean urine. I strapped it on like a jockstrap, keeping the synthetic urine at the right temperature with hand warmers.

I had become a master manipulator.

Chasing Stability Through Success

As my work performance declined, I frequently clashed with my boss. But despite the tension, he saw potential in me. He encouraged me to consider enrolling in a master's program, believing that my bachelor's degree in management, along with my decent grades at NKU, might be enough to gain acceptance.

Once again, I felt my marriage slipping away. And once again, I grasped for something—anything—to prove I was still worth staying for.

I signed up for the GMAT placement test and applied for the MBA program at NKU. The Dean of Admissions was hesitant to accept me, so we met for coffee at the campus Starbucks. I assured him—practically begged him—to give me a chance.

That promise I made to him ended up becoming a driving force behind my eventual graduation. But there were many obstacles between that meeting and my diploma, and some of them nearly derailed me completely.

I was overjoyed when I was accepted. I rushed to share the news with my wife, convinced that this time, things would finally get better. At least that's what I told myself.

Beneath my optimism, I was still drowning in the weight of my secrets—the guilt, the shame, the unbearable burden of the affair I had yet to confess.

CHAPTER 6

JUGGLING MASKS

I carried a litany of titles—employee, grad student, military veteran, husband, father, drug addict. Though the last title wasn't officially accepted by me or others at this point, it was certainly true.

I had switched from Valium to Ativan because it had a stronger effect but a shorter half-life. At the time, I thought it was a small change, just another adjustment to keep myself going. I didn't realize that this decision would have serious repercussions later.

Then came the day everything started to unravel.

It began with a sickness. It was nothing major, just a fever and some chills, enough to justify a trip to the emergency room at the Cincinnati VA. I sat under the harsh fluorescent lights, feeling the itch of withdrawal creeping in as I waited. My leg bounced restlessly, and my fingers drummed against the chair's armrest. I needed to get in, get checked, and get out.

Step 4

When I was finally in an examination room, a nurse in blue scrubs ran through the standard protocol—temperature, blood pressure, a few routine questions. Then she said, "We're going to take some blood, just to run tests."

I nodded, trying to appear nonchalant, but my heart started pounding. Blood work meant a toxicology report. And a toxicology report meant my secret life was about to be exposed.

I should have walked out. I should have come up with some excuse and left before someone stuck a needle in my arm. But I was too sick and too exhausted to think clearly.

By the time I realized what I had done, it was too late.

A few days later, my phone rang. It was my prescribing doctor. I answered, already knowing what was coming.

"Your toxicology report came back," she said, her voice firm. "You tested positive for marijuana."

My throat went dry. "Yeah, I uh—"

"We talked about this," she interrupted. "You knew the conditions. I can't continue prescribing Vicodin."

My stomach twisted into knots. This wasn't just bad news; it was a crisis. My body depended on those pills. Without them, withdrawal would hit me like a freight train.

"Please," I started, but she was done. The line went dead.

Panic set in. I needed a plan—fast.

That was the moment I started doctor shopping.

I became an actor, perfecting my performance in waiting rooms across the city. I rehearsed my stories and practiced the wincing; the slow, deliberate movements; the desperate explanations about my back pain. Some doctors believed me. Some didn't.

When the doctors' visits didn't work, I turned to the streets. I called anyone who might know someone. I met people in gas station parking lots and exchanged cash for little blue pills in fast-food bathrooms. I started dealing some of my Ativan and marijuana just to keep the supply of pain meds coming.

The lines between my identities blurred. By day, I was shaking hands with professors, submitting assignments, and sitting in meetings at work, pretending I had it all together. I was smiling, nodding, and making eye contact—each movement carefully controlled to maintain the illusion.

By night, I was desperate, texting dealers in code, driving through back roads with my pulse hammering and my eyes darting to the rearview mirror, praying I wouldn't get pulled over.

If I walked into a room sober, I felt like a fraud—a hollow, twitchy, anxious mess of a man. But if I took enough pills, I could wear the mask a little longer.

The pressure was mounting. My marriage was slipping through my fingers again. I could feel my wife pulling away, her patience wearing thin. Every time she was one foot out the door, I scrambled to find something to prove I was still worth believing in.

And then there was another miracle.

I got hired at Wright-Patterson Air Force Base as a program manager.

It felt life-changing—a real job, a fresh start, a chance to turn things around.

But deep down, I knew the truth.

I was a man running from a storm, refusing to turn around and face the wreckage I had left behind.

CHAPTER 7

FIRST BIG SCARE

The tail end of my Ativan prescription was always a nerve-wracking time. I never knew exactly when my refill would arrive in the mail, and that uncertainty gnawed at me. Every trip to the mailbox felt like a roll of the dice. Would today be the day, or would I be left stranded without Ativan?

By Friday afternoon, I was down to my last pill. I swallowed it dry, hoping it would last me through the night. I had a few Roxicodone left, and I told myself they'd be enough to carry me through. But deep down, I knew better.

That night, as my wife and son slept peacefully in the next room, my body betrayed me. It started with a subtle twitch in my fingers and a slight jerk in my arm. Then an uncontrollable shudder rippled through my body like an electric current. My muscles spasmed without warning, each tremor more violent than the last.

Panic gripped me. I stumbled to the garage, fumbling for

my hidden weed stash. Maybe, just maybe, it would calm my nervous system enough to make it stop. I took a deep inhale, holding the smoke in my lungs as if it could somehow anchor me. But relief never came.

Back inside, I tried to focus on something to distract myself. I grabbed a black ceramic bowl from the cabinet and poured in some Frosted Mini-Wheats, my hands shaking so badly that milk splashed onto the counter. I wiped it up with a paper towel, pretending it was nothing.

But as I turned down the hallway, carrying my bowl of cereal, my body suddenly seized. My arms flung outward in a violent jolt, and the bowl shot from my hands. The ceramic exploded into shards against the hardwood floor. My vision went white. My breath hitched. My body convulsed.

Then, nothing.

The next thing I remember, I was lying on a gurney, fluorescent hospital lights flickering above me as I was rushed through the emergency room doors. Muffled voices buzzed around me, but I couldn't piece together what was happening.

"Do you take any medications?" a voice finally cut through the haze.

I tried to answer, but my mouth was dry, my tongue thick like it had been stuffed with cotton. I swallowed hard.

"I take . . . Ativan," I rasped. "Two milligrams. Four times a day."

A doctor leaned over me, his face grim. "Your withdrawal from Ativan caused a seizure," he said. "Benzodiazepine withdrawal can be life-threatening."

First Big Scare

The words barely registered. All I knew was that they had to give me Ativan to stabilize my system. The drug that had nearly killed me was now the only thing keeping me alive.

When I got home, the weight of what had happened pressed down on me. My wife looked shaken, like she had seen a ghost. I could see it in her eyes—the fear, the helplessness. She had woken up to find me convulsing, and she was completely powerless to stop it.

For most people, that would have been a wake-up call. That would have been the moment they decided enough was enough. But not me.

The very next day, my Ativan refill arrived in the mail.

As I tore open the package, my hands trembled—not from withdrawal this time but from excitement. It felt like Christmas morning. Relief. Salvation.

I couldn't see the wreckage I was leaving in my wake. I couldn't see the pain in my wife's eyes, the trauma I was forcing her to endure. All I could see were those little pills in my hand.

And that was all that mattered.

CHAPTER 8

EMPLOYMENT PROBLEMS AND CAR CRASHES

Starting a career in the federal government comes with a certain prestige. The pay is great, the benefits are unbeatable, and people respect you when they hear about your job. That respect became another layer of my identity crisis. On the surface, I was a program manager for the United States Air Force, and I made sure to say it with just the right amount of pride. But on the inside, I knew the truth. I was an addict who was barely keeping it together.

Mornings became a ritual of self-medication—Ativan to keep the anxiety at bay, coffee to stay alert, 10 mg of Roxicodone to smooth it all out. When that cocktail wasn't enough, I added marijuana to the mix. At first, it worked. I would glide into the office high, floating through the day without a care. But when my supply ran low, the high was replaced with paranoia.

I felt exposed, like everyone around me could see through the polished government title to the addict underneath.

My supervisors began to take note. My arrival times were inconsistent, and my two-hour lunch breaks were raising eyebrows. What they didn't know was that I was speeding from Dayton to Cincinnati to buy pills and then smuggling them onto a military base, a federal crime that could have landed me behind bars for years. But addiction doesn't acknowledge consequences. It only acknowledges the next dose.

I knew I was one mistake away from losing my job. I needed to start arriving on time. But instead of waking up earlier, I decided to drive faster. It made perfect sense to my addict brain.

The First Crash

The morning after Alabama beat Clemson in the 2015 football national championship game, I found myself racing through the snow, desperate to shave off a few minutes from my commute. My first stop was B&B Carryout & Diner in Waynesville, Ohio, for a Big Bo BJ breakfast sandwich. As I sped through the icy roads, my car lost traction. The next thing I knew, I was skidding into a guardrail. Metal crunched. The car jolted to a stop.

I took a deep breath, assessing the damage. It wasn't too bad, so it shouldn't ruin my morning. The snowfall was heavy, so maybe no one saw it happen. I shrugged it off, grabbed my sandwich, and got back on the road.

Traffic on I-675 was a nightmare. My impatience got the best of me, and I attempted a reckless lane change to make up lost time. The tires lost their grip. The car spun. And just like that, I was fishtailing into a ditch.

Embarrassment hit harder than fear. The snow was still coming down, and I was in no hurry to face reality. So I popped a couple more Ativan, reclined my seat, and took a nap right there in the driver's seat.

When the ambulance arrived, they assumed I was unconscious. I went along with it, which made for a better story—something I could use to get out of trouble at work. And it worked. A hospital visit, a doctor's note, a "poor pitiful me" routine later, and my job was safe.

I'm sure my wife was horrified. But she stayed. After everything, she stayed.

The Second Crash

Later that year, there was another frantic morning and another dose of Ativan and Roxicodone. But there was no time to smoke before leaving the house. So I packed my vape and planned to sneak a few hits on the way to work.

I rarely took that risk. Marijuana has a distinct smell, and getting caught with it while entering a military base would have been a disaster. But that day, I convinced myself it was worth it.

Speeding northbound on I-75, I barely noticed the slick roads. My mind was locked onto my mission: make up for lost time. Then suddenly, the tires lost contact with the pavement. The car started to hydroplane.

I yanked the wheel, trying to regain control. For a brief second, I thought I had it.

Then, *Boom!*

A semi-truck plowed into the driver's side of my car at full speed.

Everything went black.

I don't remember the impact. I don't remember the airbag going off. But when I came to, I was staring up at the sky through a shattered windshield. I didn't ask myself, *Am I alive? Am I hurt?* I asked, *Where's my vape?*

Instinct took over. Before doing anything else, I reached down, grabbed the vape, and stuffed it deep into my left sock. Getting caught with paraphernalia was a bigger concern to me than the fact that I had just been T-boned by a semi-truck.

I turned my head and locked eyes with the truck driver. She was frozen in shock. Her face was pale. She thought I was dead.

I needed to show her I wasn't. I reached for the driver's side door to step out, but it wouldn't budge. It was crushed beyond repair. Without thinking, I slammed my shoulder into it only to be met with a sharp, searing pain. I gritted my teeth and scrambled out through the passenger side instead.

As I stood next to the wreckage, my heart was pounding, but not from fear. It was something else. It was a sick, twisted feeling of invincibility.

You can't kill me, I thought. *Not even a semi-truck can kill me.*

The ambulance arrived, but I argued against going to the hospital. "I have to get to work," I insisted. They ignored me and strapped me onto a stretcher.

In the emergency room, I found myself facing a new kind of anxiety, not from the accident but from the state trooper standing at the foot of my bed, waiting for my toxicology report. I could feel my pant leg slightly riding up, exposing the outline of the vaporizer stuffed in my sock. If he looked down, I was done.

Minutes felt like hours.

Then finally he handed me a ticket for reckless driving and walked out.

I had dodged another bullet.

The Aftermath

My wife picked me up, looking exhausted—emotionally, mentally, and physically drained. We drove straight to the junkyard to sign over the car title.

A worker at the junkyard led us to the wreckage. Seeing it up close sent a chill through me. The car was mangled beyond recognition. The worker studied it for a moment before turning to me.

"Who was driving this?" she asked.

"I was."

Her eyebrows lifted. "We were sure the driver didn't survive."

I should have recognized the weight of her words. I should have felt lucky, grateful.

But instead, all I felt was nothing.

I reported back to work the next day with a doctor's note and another dramatic story. I told it with pride like I was made of steel. Sure, my shoulder was sore, but after taking on a semi-truck at highway speeds, who wouldn't be sore?

Two days later, my body told a different story.

I was struggling to breathe at work, but I had cried wolf too many times to take myself seriously. I toughed it out until the end of the day, and then I called my wife.

"I think something's wrong," I told her. "I need to go to the hospital."

If I were her, I would have assumed it was just another excuse to chase pain meds. But this time, it wasn't.

A doctor at the VA ran tests and gave me the news. I had a lacerated spleen. It was either going to heal itself or rupture. If it ruptured, I'd need emergency surgery.

I spent three days in the ICU, my wife by my side watching over me like she had so many times before. By some miracle, my spleen healed on its own. I walked away from yet another disaster, seemingly untouched.

But the real wounds—the ones I was ignoring—were only getting deeper.

CHAPTER 9

MOM'S PASSING

The Dilaudid drip and prescription meds put me right back into my opiate addiction. I had some time off work due to the severity of my injury, and my plan was to take the medicine—5 mg of Roxicodone four times a day—exactly as prescribed.

That plan didn't last long. Before I knew it, I was crushing and snorting them.

As the prescription bottle emptied, fear and anxiety gripped me. I knew what was coming—withdrawals. Desperation took over, and I reached out to my dealer. The cycle of addiction had me in its grip once again.

A week later, I was back in the office, high on pills I had bought off the street. But in my addicted mind, I felt good about it. I wasn't increasing my doses, so I convinced myself that this time I had control.

One night after work, I got a call from my cousin Robert who had just been released from prison. My mom loved

Step 4

Robert like he was her own, and I thought it would be a great surprise to take him to see her at work.

My mom was a server at the Seasons 52 restaurant in Cincinnati. When we walked in, she lit up, beaming from ear to ear.

"I'm about to get cut," she said, meaning her shift was almost over.

"We'll head over to the Pilot Inn," I told her. "Meet us there when you're done."

Robert and I went ahead and played a few games of pool. After a while, Mom walked in, and we ordered a round of shots and a beer.

Ironically, I was trying to be responsible that night. After finishing my drink, I said my goodbyes and went home to rest up for another long day at work.

The next morning, I woke up exhausted. I was sure the alcohol had played a part, but I grabbed a few pills from my pocket, hoping they'd help me push through the day. Instead of giving me energy, they made me even more tired.

I remember nodding off at my desk when my phone rang. It was my Uncle Jeff. He lived with my mom at the time. The moment I saw his name on my screen, a wave of unease washed over me.

"Hello?" I answered.

His voice was frantic and shaky. "Your mom is dead!"

The world around me collapsed. I lost it right there in my cubicle. My coworkers stopped and stared, but I couldn't care less.

Mom's Passing

A kind woman from the office rushed over. "What happened?"

"My mom died," I choked out.

"I'm so sorry," she said softly, offering comfort I could barely feel.

She insisted on driving me to my family. By the time I arrived, Mom was already gone. I never got to see her one last time. That reality cut deeper than I could express. I felt numb.

My mom had lived a hard life, and I had always wanted to be the one to help her through it. It felt like my mission in life was to give her hope, to show her that we could break free from pain and disappointment. And now that mission was over.

I had failed.

Looking back, I realize now that so much of what I had chased—college degrees and achievements—hadn't been for me. They had been for her. I wanted to show her that anything was possible. And now she was gone.

For the first time, I truly looked in the mirror and faced my addiction—not just the using but the empty purpose that had been driving me all along. Without her, what was I even fighting for?

I knew something had to change or I was going to spiral beyond return.

That's when I found the courage to reach out.

I called a man I deeply respected—Randy. I kept it surface-level at first. "Mom passed away," I said. "I'm not in a good place." I asked if we could meet, and he invited me to his house.

It was the day we buried my mom. Randy lived only a few minutes from the cemetery. When I told my wife about the meeting, she hesitated.

"We should be with your family at your aunt and uncle's," she said.

But I insisted. Something inside me knew I had to go to Randy's first. When we arrived, my wife stayed inside with Randy's wife while Randy and I went for a walk.

As we walked, I told Randy the truth—the whole truth.

"I've been abusing pain pills," I admitted.

He asked me tough questions. "How are you using them?"

I hesitated and then forced the words out. "I'm snorting them."

He was evaluating me, trying to see if I was being honest. Looking back, I know that conversation was divinely orchestrated. On my own, I wasn't capable of that level of honesty. But God made sure I was truthful.

When we got back to Randy's house, we stopped in the driveway.

Randy looked me in the eyes. "Well, what are you asking me, Brandon?"

For the first time in my life, I had the courage to say it.

"Help," I said, my voice shaking, tears streaming down my face. "I'm asking for help."

Why is that word so hard for a man to say?

Randy didn't hesitate.

"I'd be honored," he said.

If you're reading this, take notes on that response. It's powerful.

He told me he needed to talk to his wife and would get back to me on what help would look like.

My wife and I left to be with my family, the weight of my mom's passing still heavy. The ride was quiet. The air between us felt different, like something was shifting.

For the first time in a long time, I felt like real change was possible.

CHAPTER 10

AN HONEST ATTEMPT AT SOBRIETY

Randy and his wife offered me a place to stay indefinitely—but with conditions. I had to get up every morning and go with Randy where he worked at Southbrook Christian Church in Miamisburg, Ohio. I agreed. I talked it over with my wife, and just like that, the journey to sobriety began.

At the time, the only medication I was prescribed was Ritalin for ADHD. I was upfront with Randy and his wife about it because I was beginning to understand the value of honesty. Randy, a counselor, gave me a few weeks to detox. He also spoke with my supervisors at the Air Force Base and explained that I needed counseling after my mother's passing. I told him the truth, that if my job knew I had relapsed, I'd be fired. He made it clear that he wouldn't lie for me, but he promised to handle the conversation carefully, keeping the details minimal. To this day, I respect that decision.

Before heading to Randy's house, I finished off the last of my 10 mg of Roxicodone that had been a final crutch to get me through my mom's visitation and funeral. I wanted to be honest from that moment forward, so I admitted to using but assured them I had no more pills left.

The next morning, we went to Southbrook Christian Church. I managed to get through the day, but my Ritalin prescription bottle sat in my bag, practically screaming at me. I took my doses as prescribed, but the temptation to take more was already creeping in.

By day two, the withdrawal hit hard. Randy counseled me between his other appointments, and I did my best to give him the energy he deserved, but it was draining every ounce of me.

On day three, I couldn't do it. I told Randy I wasn't able to go with him to the church. My sister lived nearby, so we came up with a plan. I would rest in her guest bedroom for the day. This was the peak of my withdrawal. Lying in that bed, my body shaking and my mind racing, all I could think was *I can't do this.*

That evening, Randy picked me up, and I felt like a failure. The only thing I could think of to ease the pain was more Ritalin.

At that point, I had accepted that opiates were killing me. I had mentally and physically written them off. But I didn't see overmedicating on Ritalin as a problem. It wasn't the same, I told myself. It wasn't as bad.

By day four, I started sneaking into the church bathroom to snort them.

An Honest Attempt at Sobriety

By day six, I had a full routine of abusing Ritalin just enough to take the edge off the opiate withdrawal. It wasn't obvious to others, and that made it easier to justify. I convinced myself that I was on the right track.

Nine months passed without opiates. To the outside world, I was sober. People had hope in me, and for the most part, I felt like I was getting better.

But my addiction hadn't disappeared. It had just changed shape.

And soon, everything was about to fall apart

CHAPTER 11

A NEW LOW

Training classes were a routine part of my job with the federal government. Most of the training was computer-based, but as a program manager, I was also required to attend in-person coursework to keep my position. One particular class was held in a massive lecture hall with 300 to 500 students—military officers in uniform and civilians like me in business attire.

My supervisor had stressed the importance of arriving on time. He mentioned that being late meant I wouldn't be allowed to participate, but the details were hazy. I had convinced my psychiatrist that I needed to be back on Ativan. I thought I could take the same amounts as I was taking long before. The Ativan had started to erode my memory.

Determined not to be late, I got to the base early. But I had no idea where the lecture hall was. I wandered through the building, growing frantic. The last thing I remember from that day was ducking into a bathroom, panic rising in my chest. To silence it, I took a couple more Ativan.

I must have found my way to class, but I have no memory of it.

The next morning, I woke up to a text from an unfamiliar number.

"Are you okay?" it said.

Concerned, I called back. A woman answered.

"Do you remember me?" she asked.

"Not really," I admitted.

"I was in class with you yesterday. I'm an officer in the Air Force, and you were pretty out of it."

I felt my stomach drop. I stayed on the call just long enough to gauge how bad it was. When I sensed I hadn't done anything illegal, I got off the phone, shaken. Had I passed out? Mumbled nonsense? Embarrassed myself in front of a room full of professionals? To this day, I still don't know.

That weekend, my wife left for a women's trip with her family and friends. I assumed I'd be staying home with our three-year-old son, but she had made other arrangements. She left him with her father instead.

She didn't trust me to take care of our own child.

The realization burned. I spent the weekend alone, numbing myself with pills and aimlessly roaming Cincinnati. By Saturday night, I ended up at a mechanic's shop in Norwood, a familiar escape when my wife distanced herself from me.

On Sunday morning, I woke up to more texts.

"You drove to the shop with all four doors of your Malibu wide open."

I had blacked out again. It was another stretch of time erased, another reminder that I was spiraling.

When my wife and son returned home, she was livid.

"I can't believe you called my mom and dad to ask where our son was," she said.

I had no memory of making that call.

The Intervention

Monday morning, I got up for work, still clinging to the routine. I reached for my Ativan bottle and was startled by how few were left. I popped a couple, cleaned up, and made my way downstairs.

But instead of heading out the door, I walked into an ambush.

Three men stood in my living room—my Uncle Brian, a man of unwavering faith; Randy, who had kindly volunteered to help me; and my direct supervisor from Wright-Patterson Air Force Base.

It was 7:30 in the morning, and this was an intervention.

I don't remember everything that was said, but one sentence cut through the fog: "If you don't go to the Cincinnati VA treatment center, you no longer have a job."

My supervisor mentioned the incident in the lecture hall, how I had been so incoherent that people had called him at work. Shame and guilt crashed over me. If I lost my job, I lost my wife. And I couldn't afford to lose her.

So I agreed, reluctantly.

I was told I'd be admitted to the psych ward until a bed opened up in the substance abuse program. They said it would be a few days. That was a lie.

I spent over three weeks in the psych ward and grew bitter.

Rock Bottom

While I was in rehab, my wife called.

"I need the car insurance information," she said.

"Why?" I asked.

"Because I'm switching my car insurance," she explained.

And just like that, I knew. She was leaving—for good.

"Don't do this. Not while I'm in here," I begged.

My pleas were desperate and selfish. I wasn't thinking about everything I had put her through—only about what I was losing.

After that call, my focus shifted from recovery to survival. I stopped caring about getting better. I did just enough to complete the program and keep my job. But in my mind, the second I got out, I was going on a warpath.

I tried to distract myself by flirting with women in Alcoholics Anonymous (AA)—shallow attempts to convince myself I could move on. But the hollowness inside me only deepened.

One day, I got into a heated argument with a staff member. He made this offhand comment: "I called your sister last night."

I snapped. I tore into him, threatening his job and demanding consequences. I wasn't angry at him. I was just spewing out all the poison I had been swallowing for months—the affair, the addiction, my wife leaving me. He just happened to be the match that lit the fuse.

It turned into a clinic-wide scandal. The board held multiple meetings on how to handle the situation. In the end, they landed on a compromise. I would "graduate" from the program two weeks early. The staff member would keep his job.

The Relapse

My wife still had my car, so she and my son picked me up. In my mind, that meant we were getting back together.

But when we pulled up to the house, it was staged for sale. The furniture was gone. That hit me like a train. *I'm homeless.*

I made a move toward my wife. She rejected me. And in that moment, I finally understood that she was done.

I got out of the car, and she drove away with our son. I stood there holding a duffel bag with no clue of where to go.

Then I remembered the vape and weed stashed in the garage. Thirty minutes out of treatment, and I was already high.

Too ashamed to call family, I met up with a guy from rehab. We went to J. Alexander's restaurant, blew $500 on food and drinks, and made plans with the bartender to meet her in downtown Cincinnati.

Hours later, I was behind the wheel, drunk and high, blasting Drake as I pulled into the crowded bar district.

I found a narrow parking spot and backed in, straight into a Jaguar. A woman in the passenger seat jumped out and got her boyfriend. He confronted me, demanding cash. Then he reached under the car seat and pulled out a gun.

"You're giving me cash. Even if we have to go to the ATM."

I was terrified, but I played it cool. I walked with him to the ATM, intentionally entering the wrong PIN and stalling. Eventually, I slipped away.

The guy from rehab had abandoned me the second the gun came out. Alone, drunk, and reckless, I wandered back into the night.

I was four hours out of treatment and already in freefall.

CHAPTER 12

DEPRESSION

I drove from the bar district to the apartment of a woman I met in AA. The next morning, desperate and ashamed, I hinted at moving in with her. She dodged the idea. And in that moment, I felt smaller than ever. I had nowhere to go.

It was Saturday morning, and I was due back at the base on Monday. With 48 hours left before I had to face reality, I swallowed my pride and called my dad. The conversation was tough. I had to admit that my wife had left me and I was homeless. To my relief, he and my stepmom understood. They offered me a place to stay until I could find something more stable.

The drive from Cincinnati to Waynesville where they lived felt heavy. My guilt and shame rode in the back of the car. But my biggest burden was the fact that I had to report to work with marijuana in my system. I was convinced they would drug test me immediately and that I'd be fired for good.

By the grace of God, they didn't.

Instead, when I arrived on Monday, I sat through a few brief meetings. Then I was told, "We need to find a program for you to work on. Until then, you can work remotely from home. Focus on your computer-based training modules."

It was music to my ears.

I had spent the entire weekend dreading termination. Instead, I had a lifeline—a chance to work from my dad's house and avoid the guilt and shame of relapsing hours after treatment while facing people who had given me every opportunity to turn my life around.

What I didn't realize was that isolation would be its own kind of hell.

At first, I did the bare minimum to keep my job. But as the days passed, I found myself sinking deeper into self-pity. My thoughts consumed me. I had lost everything—my wife, my son, my house. All I had left was my car and my job.

Looking back, I should have been grateful for those things. But depression doesn't work like that. When you're in it, gratitude feels impossible.

My dad and stepmom gave me a place to stay, but I barely existed in their home. I locked myself in my room for days. Instead of taking advantage of my second chance at work, I buried myself under the covers and avoided the world.

I placed my work laptop at the foot of my bed, positioned the mouse just right, and kicked it with my foot every so often to keep my online status active.

I sensed my dad's frustration. He knew I was struggling,

but he held back the lectures. I was distant, and my presence brought a negative energy into their home. But I was too deep in my own misery to care.

On the surface, I was still "successful." I had a title—program manager in the Air Force. I had money. I used those things to build an alter ego, convincing myself that as long as I had those labels, no one could judge me.

But inside, I was dying.

I was abstaining from drugs but used alcohol occasionally. I played flag football with some friends, which helped for a time. But Ritalin was becoming a problem. Paranoia set in. I isolated more. Every time I felt "off," my instinct was to take more.

Conversations with my dad became tense. I resented some of his comments, which pushed me farther into isolation. I started looking for my own place. I was making enough to buy a house, so I reached out to a Realtor.

Then work assigned me to a flight simulator program, which meant I had to go back to the base. It was a double-edged sword. On the one hand, it got me out of the house. On the other hand, the program made no sense to me. No matter how hard I tried, I couldn't find my footing. It was like being in a foreign country where I didn't speak the language.

Still, I pushed forward. I had a house lined up and was getting ready to close.

One weekend, my son Aiden came to stay with me. We opened his Christmas presents and took them to the basement to play. His favorite was a remote-control monster truck. We crashed it into every wall, laughing until our stomachs hurt.

When we were on our way to meet up with his mom, she called and said she needed more time. So we turned around and went back inside to play a little longer.

As we walked in, my dad looked up and said, "What are you two doing back? Some of us have to work tomorrow, big boy."

His words cut deep. I don't remember exactly how I responded, but whatever I said made my dad snap. He jumped up from his seat, got in my face, and pushed me as I stood on a basement step. I caught myself on the guardrail, injuring my hand. I shoved him back. Then I turned and saw my son burst into tears and run.

Instinct kicked in. I ran after Aiden. He was hiding behind a chair, sobbing.

Even now, as I write this, I feel the anger rise.

In that moment, something in me broke.

Why am I even trying?

After I dropped Aiden off with his mom, I made up my mind right then and there to drive straight to Cincinnati to get pills.

And just like that, I was off to the races again.

This time, things were about to get really bad.

CHAPTER 13

NEW HOME

Closing on my new house should have been a fresh start, a new beginning. Instead, it felt like the beginning of the end. Excitement and fear waged war inside me. I was relieved to finally have my own place and no longer be a burden to my dad and his wife, especially after the stair incident—the breaking point for both of us. But I was also terrified because despite my best intentions, I was already back on pain pills.

My cousins Kyle and Robert helped move my furniture into my new house. I snorted a few 10 mg Roxicodones before picking up the U-Haul, thinking it would help me push through the day. Instead, my mind was hijacked. During the entire move, I wasn't thinking about the house, the furniture, or my future. I was consumed with one thought—withdrawal was coming, and if I didn't get more pills, I would drown in it.

I was out of pills. I told myself I wouldn't get more.

But as soon as my cousins left, I made the call.

This is the last time, I lied to myself. Deep down, I knew I was at a crossroads—sink or swim—but addiction never lets you choose so easily.

Determined to convince myself I was still in control, I started reaching out to my dealers for Adderall. I told myself that if Ritalin had helped me get off opiates before, then Adderall would do the trick this time.

Oh, what twisted logic.

The first time, Ritalin had worked because there was structure, some level of honesty at least to everyone but myself. This time, I was in full-blown denial, hiding my addiction from everyone. Three days into my new home, I was free from opiates but high on ridiculous amounts of Adderall and Ritalin. My muscles were stiff, my body was exhausted, and my mind was in chaos. I hadn't slept in days.

Desperate for more, I called my dealer.

"You got any Adderall?" I asked.

"Nah, man," he said.

Paranoia and exhaustion were crashing down on me. I needed anything to take the edge off.

"What else you got?" I asked.

"I got some blues."

Blues were 30 mg Roxicodone, the strongest Percocet I had ever found on the street.

"How much?" I asked him.

"Thirty bucks a pill."

"Let me have four."

Half an hour later, I met him outside my house, grabbed the pills, went inside, and crushed one. The moment I snorted that first line, everything changed. The cycle of destruction had locked me back in, tighter than ever.

The pills were too expensive to maintain for long, but I couldn't stop. The combination of Ritalin, Adderall, and 30 mg Roxicodone made me feel invincible. At work, I sneaked into the bathroom to snort the crushed up pills. I kept meeting with Randy for counseling at the church, but the shame of my addiction kept me silent. I even started an early morning workout routine with my brother and a friend, hoping that maybe, just maybe, I could outrun this.

But every morning still started the same—a minimum of 10 mg of Adderall to get me moving.

The stimulants made me feel speedy all the time. My body was breaking down, my appetite was gone, and my clothes were getting loose. I was fading, and people were starting to notice.

So I came up with a brilliant plan—steroids. If I took steroids, I'd gain muscle, look healthy, and fool everyone into thinking I had it all together.

I started taking Trenabol and Test 400. The first shot went into my right shoulder. My plan was to hit the gym right after, but the pain was unbearable, and my whole arm was useless. For three days, I couldn't even think about another injection. On the fourth day, I worked up the nerve to try again, this time in my glute. The pain was still there, but I was mobile. I made it to the gym, and the results were immediate. My strength skyrocketed.

I was now on Ritalin, Adderall, Roxicodone, and two steroids.

I was getting bigger—so big that my suit pants barely fit. I had to walk carefully at work, afraid a wrong step would split my slacks right down the seam. I started drawing attention from women, but I couldn't let anyone close enough to see the truth. I was a fraud, and I knew it.

The drugs kept the mask on, just enough to survive.

At the gym and at work, I could distract myself from the misery. But when I was alone at home, the suicidal thoughts came in waves. I remember sitting in my bathroom, needle in hand, torn between injecting another round of steroids or throwing it away and settling into my normal depression.

I chose the needle.

The changes in my body were undeniable—bigger muscles, insane strength—but none of it mattered when I looked in the mirror. The reflection staring back at me was a man I could no longer stand to see.

CHAPTER 14

LOSING MORE

With my addiction draining me faster than I could keep up, I started opening my home to other drug addicts. It wasn't charity; it was survival. Keeping drugs close meant I never had to go without.

I let a relative and his girlfriend move into my basement. They were both IV drug users, and through them, I was introduced to the world of shooting up. They primarily used meth and fentanyl, two drugs I swore I would never touch.

I remember the first time I was offered meth. I declined, trying to convince myself I had boundaries. Another time, I crushed up a line of Ritalin, passed it off as meth, and snorted it in front of them just to shut them up. In my mind, meth and fentanyl were drug addict drugs, as if I wasn't one myself. I still had the illusion of control.

I wrecked my car again, this time straight into a telephone pole. The insurance claim was a disaster, but eventually it got sorted and I sent the car to a body shop. In the meantime, I rented a car to get to work.

One night, while I was asleep, my relative and his girlfriend stole the rental from my garage and went on a drug run. I had no idea. The next morning, I got ready for work, walked outside, and the car was gone.

Panic hit me immediately. I grabbed my phone, ready to call my supervisor, but before I could dial, I noticed a text from my Aunt Kelly.

"Call me immediately."

I dialed her number.

"Robert overdosed last night. The cops took your rental car."

I sat in silence for a moment and then muttered, "Let me call you back. I need to call work."

When I got my supervisor on the line, I kept the details vague, but I could hear it in his voice that he was done with me.

"Let me get my supervisor. We're coming to your house," he said.

I sat at my kitchen table, waiting. At first, I assumed they were picking me up for work. But when they arrived, they didn't offer me a ride. Instead, they came inside, sat down, and started asking questions.

I told them the truth.

When they left, I had no idea what to expect. The fact that they didn't take me to work made my stomach drop. I started to panic.

Losing More

Then the call came.

I was fired.

In just a short span of time, I had lost everything—my wife, my son, my car, and now my job. The only thing I had left was my house, and with no income, I wasn't sure how much longer I could keep that either.

The next day, my cousin's girlfriend, still wearing a hospital gown, showed up in a sheriff's car. Within hours of arriving, she called a friend to bring her fentanyl. She was sick.

I watched as she and her friend sat at my dining room table, cooking the powder, tying off, and pushing the needle into their veins.

"I can't believe this is my life," I thought to myself.

A few days later, I was the one in withdrawal. I was sick, desperate, and calling around for pills with no luck. The only lead I had was a girl who was going to Dayton. She said her dealer sometimes had pills.

It was my only hope.

She picked me up, and we drove to the dealer. I sat in the passenger seat while she went inside. Every second felt like an eternity. When she finally came back, she gave me the news.

"He doesn't have pills."

I slumped in my seat, feeling like my body was shutting down. I was too sick to argue, too sick to think.

She pulled into a gas station, somehow got needles, and got back in the car.

As she prepped her shot, I found myself asking about fentanyl. "What's it like?"

"It's the best high ever," she said. Then, almost as an afterthought, she added, "But you shouldn't try it. It's hard to get off."

I was too far gone to care.

"Will it make me feel better?"

"Oh yeah."

The next thing I remember was water splashing in my face. Someone was yelling at me. My vision was blurred, and I was trying to focus.

"You overdosed," someone said.

I was in my garage. I had no idea how I got there. My body felt heavy like I had been dragged through hell. I stumbled inside my house, made it to my bedroom, and collapsed inches from my bed.

I fell back into overdose.

When I came to, two girls were smacking my face.

"You were dead," one of them said.

"Was I?" I murmured.

"Yeah, bro. You OD'd."

I looked over at my nightstand. Sitting there was the folded paper the fentanyl had come in.

The girl who had shot me up had called her mom when I went out. Her mom came to my house and threw water in my face. Then they both took off, leaving the drugs behind in case I died so they could come back and take whatever I didn't use.

This was the reality of addiction.

The two girls still in my house were giddy when they realized I had fentanyl strong enough to kill.

They couldn't wait to try it.

CHAPTER 15

ANOTHER ATTEMPT AT REHAB

The two girls used up all the fentanyl, and I felt the withdrawal creeping in—cold sweats, aching bones, a familiar panic. I kept calling my usual dealers, but no one answered. The girls I was with claimed they knew someone in Dayton, so we piled into my car and headed out.

When we got to their dealer's house, they went inside while I waited in the car. They came back out with way fewer pills than they'd promised. Typical. In the world of addiction, everyone looks out for themselves first.

Back at my house, the tension boiled over. I demanded to know why I got shorted and why I wasn't getting any money back. One of the girls started yelling at me, and I snapped.

"You're not welcome here anymore," I told her.

She scoffed and demanded the food she'd bought. It was a single 2-liter bottle of Mountain Dew in my fridge. I grabbed it and hurled it across the room. That was the last I saw of her. I had no idea where she went or even how she had gotten there.

I had just enough pills to get me through the night, but I knew tomorrow would be hell. Desperate, I kept calling my dealer in Cincinnati. Nothing. The withdrawal loomed over me like a storm cloud. Then my phone rang. It was my wife.

"I want to bring our son to see you tomorrow," she said.

My heart leapt. "That would be great."

But I knew I couldn't face my son in withdrawal. I needed more pills. I called my dealer over and over, terrified of what would happen if I was sick the next day. I took my last pill and went to bed, praying for a callback.

The Intervention

The next morning, my phone finally buzzed. My dealer had re-upped. Relief flooded me. I ordered 20 pills for $200 and hit the road. One of the girls was still at my house. She begged to come along, desperate for fentanyl.

"My guy doesn't have fentanyl," I told her. "And I need to get back before my son arrives."

She still pleaded, so I let her ride along but made no promises. We got to Cincinnati, and I got my pills. I crushed a couple and snorted them in the car before heading back. She was whining the whole way, begging me to stop in Dayton. But traffic was brutal, and time was running out.

"My wife and son will be at my house any minute," I told her. "I can't miss this."

She was upset but accepted it. As we pulled into my garage, I gave her strict instructions.

"Go to the basement. Hide in the room on the left. Lock the door and don't open it for anyone."

She disappeared downstairs just as I looked out the front window. My wife's car pulled up, followed by a caravan of vehicles. One by one, 20 to 30 family members and friends filed into my house.

Another intervention.

I should've felt loved. Instead, I felt ambushed.

"How dare they," I thought.

My aunt spoke first. "Now that we know you're not working, we think it's time for treatment."

I clenched my right hand in my pocket, gripping my bag of pills. I wasn't ready. Not yet. I had enough to last a couple of days.

My friend Josh started packing my bags. It was clear that I had no choice.

Randy, another friend, pleaded with me. "Just go, man. Do this."

If I hadn't been high, I might have surrendered right there. But in that moment, all I wanted was another hit. My mind raced. My house was flooded with people. My shame was suffocating, and there was a random girl hiding in my basement. I felt trapped. The only way out was to say yes.

Beckett Springs

That night, I stayed at Randy's house. The next morning, they drove me to Beckett Springs treatment center. I walked in high.

"Do you have any drugs on you?" the intake nurse asked.

"No," I lied.

They explained they had a strict search policy. My stomach twisted. "Where's the nearest bathroom?" I asked.

They pointed me in the right direction. I locked myself in a stall and snorted the rest of my stash. If I was going in, I was going in on a high.

The next morning, the withdrawal hit like a freight train—sweating, muscle aches, restless legs, depression, anxiety, diarrhea. The comfort meds barely touched it. By day two, I was begging for Suboxone. The nurse encouraged me to push through detox without it, but I couldn't. I demanded it.

The moment I took that first dose, it was like flipping a switch. I went from bedridden to the life of the party. I introduced myself to everyone, acting like I had it all together.

My divorce was finalized while I was in treatment. I remember slipping off my wedding ring, tears streaming down my face. My heart ached, but instead of dealing with it, I distracted myself. I started flirting with a woman in treatment. By the time we were discharged, we had made plans. She was moving in with me.

Back to Reality

During my stay, my aunt and uncle brought my son to visit. It was a bright spot in the darkness. I opened up to them about childhood trauma I'd buried for years. Their reaction made it clear. Something clicked for them. I didn't know why I blurted it out, but I did. It was the first time I'd ever spoken about it, but it wouldn't be the last.

My dad visited too. For the first time in my life, I saw him cry. We had been through so much pain—his divorce, my addiction—but I had never seen him break like that. It crushed me. He tried to stay positive, but the pain in his eyes was undeniable.

The day before I was discharged, he called.

"I'll pick you up tomorrow," he said. Then his voice softened. "I have some bad news. One of your friends overdosed."

My stomach dropped. But before I could even process it, I asked, "Can you take me to Walgreens to fill my Suboxone prescription?"

He hesitated but agreed. On the way, he mentioned that my bank said I'd missed a mortgage payment. I knew I hadn't, but something about that news broke me. I felt doomed.

The Spiral

A friend got me a job before I left treatment. I was supposed to start on Monday. My new girlfriend moved in over the weekend. It didn't take long to realize we didn't even like each other. But misery loves company.

Monday came, and I started the job. By Thursday, I was fired.

I started abusing Suboxone. I spent all day in bed. I kicked my new girlfriend out and sank into months of deep depression and isolation.

Rehab hadn't saved me. I was still lost.

CHAPTER 16

LONELY

The next month was a blur of isolation and self-destruction. I was abusing my Suboxone prescription daily, hiding away from the world beneath a pile of blankets. I'd lie in bed for hours, motionless, hopeless, and numb. I wasn't working. My bills were stacking up, and I had no idea how I was going to pay them.

Even though I'd lost control, my Ritalin prescription kept showing up in the mail like clockwork. So I added that to the mix. I snorted Ritalin and popped Suboxone, chasing any feeling other than emptiness. As my Suboxone supply started to run low, I knew I didn't have enough to make it to the next refill. So I made a desperate decision. I took the rest all at once and then forced myself to go through withdrawal.

Again.

To survive the withdrawal, I leaned on Ritalin. Suboxone may have been a synthetic opioid, but Ritalin could light up my brain just enough to distract me from the darkness creeping in. But when the high wore off, the depression came back stronger and thicker, like quicksand pulling me under.

For the next three months, I did nothing. I just existed. In my mind, quitting Suboxone was the noble thing to do. But I was blind to the fact that the Ritalin addiction was quietly sinking its claws deeper into me.

Eventually, I picked up a roofing job with my cousin. I was grateful to be working again, but I was terrified. Our first job was on a steep roof, and I remember standing there frozen, heart pounding, watching the others move around like it was nothing.

I kept wondering how they were so calm. How are they functioning like this?

I got my answer soon enough.

One day at lunch, my cousin asked me for a ride to East Dayton.

"For what?" I asked.

"Just need to pick up some supplies," he said.

I drove him to a house, parked outside, and waited. When he came out, something didn't sit right. I refused to drive off until he told me the truth.

After some back and forth, he finally came clean.

"I had to pick up stuff for everybody," he admitted.

"Drugs?" I asked.

"Yeah," he said. "Some boy and some girl."

Boy and girl—heroin and cocaine.

"Let me get some coke," I said without hesitation.

Lonely

He tried to talk me out of it, but I insisted. Eventually, he pulled out a handful of capsules and handed me two. That was it—the beginning of my next downward spiral.

At the job site, the other guys acted like they liked me. They laughed with me and shared stories. But deep down, I knew the truth. I was the mule. I was the one taking all the risk, transporting their stash every day.

Then one evening after work, my car got repossessed.

Suddenly, I was no longer useful to them. Their attitude flipped overnight. I got fired not long after. I had no job and no car, and I was falling behind on my mortgage. And now I was fully hooked on both cocaine and Ritalin.

Coke was expensive—too expensive. And the loneliness in my house started to feel unbearable. I knew things were bad. I thought they couldn't get any worse.

I was wrong.

One night, someone showed up at my door with crystal meth. I didn't hesitate. I tried it.

And in that moment, everything changed.

My life was about to spiral faster and harder than anyone could have ever imagined.

CHAPTER 17

CRYSTAL METH

It didn't take long for meth to become a daily habit. I had found a dealer who moved large quantities, and in 2018, I agreed to help run the operation. One night, I picked up 13 ounces of meth, took it back to my basement, weighed it, broke it down into small bags, and spent the night delivering those bags across two counties.

I was high—too high to realize I was the one taking all the risk. If my dealer and I got pulled over, it was my car, my hands, and my name on the line. But when you're deep in addiction, risk feels irrelevant. Numbness takes over.

After we sold everything, we headed to a local casino to blow off steam. Once that thrill wore off, we went back to my house. That's when I noticed the water had been shut off.

I still had a couple bags of meth and a few bags of fentanyl left. I made a call, hopped in my car, and set out to sell enough to cover the water bill. A couple minutes into the drive, I realized a cop was tailing me. The lights turned on. I got pulled over.

I was arrested for drug possession.

While I was cuffed and booked, the task force raided my house. They flipped it upside down, looking for whatever they could find.

I spent two days in jail before being released on bond. I had no ride home, so I walked to the courthouse and stood out front, begging strangers for a lift. Eventually, a young couple agreed to take me. When I got home, the door was locked. I had to crawl through a window. Inside, the house was wrecked—ransacked. It looked like a storm had hit it. That moment struck me hard. It was a new low.

After that, I tried to slow down. I picked up a low-paying job just to keep the lights on. I was still behind on my mortgage, and the stress was eating me alive. Then a small piece of good news came through. My felony drug charges had been dropped.

It should have been a miracle, a second chance. But instead of seeing it that way, I spiraled.

I started using again.

This time, it got worse. I became more reckless, more promiscuous. I started making adult videos. Meth and marijuana were back in my daily routine. Around November of 2018, I stopped using, hoping to clean myself up before the holidays. I thought maybe I could piece my family back together. But when that reunion never happened, I completely fell apart.

I started selling and using again—meth, Xanax, marijuana, anything to numb the pain. My behavior turned darker, more violent. I was robbing drug dealers and hurting people. It was bad. Really bad.

Eventually, the bank foreclosed on my house, and I was preparing to move in with my girlfriend. That's when I got the call. It was a guy who claimed he knew a dealer who had a lot of drugs and cash. He asked if I wanted to rob him.

My answer? "Yes."

But it was a setup. The guy was working with the task force who had tailed me and pulled me over. In my car they found guns, drugs, and scales—everything they needed to seal the case. Not only was I booked on new charges but the state also reopened my old case.

Prison wasn't just likely; it was certain.

And that's exactly what happened.

I sat in that jail cell knowing my choices had finally caught up with me. There was no one else to blame. I had burned every bridge, hurt people I loved, and betrayed myself over and over again. But somewhere in the silence of that cold, concrete room, I felt the whisper of something greater—something holy—not condemnation but invitation. It was like God wasn't done with me yet. I didn't know it at the time, but prison would become the place where everything changed, where my chains—literal and spiritual—would start to break, not overnight but over time. Rock bottom wasn't the end of my story. It was the beginning of redemption.

CHAPTER 18

JAIL AND PRISON

My girlfriend bailed me out, and I went right back to selling meth. My logic was to make enough money to buy a lawyer to beat the case and then stop selling drugs.

That's not how it went.

I ended up with a warrant while I was out on bond, and after consecutive nights of being a menace, I was arrested again.

I went back to jail, this time angry. My first night, the correctional officers (COs) were passing out commissary, and I heard some guys talking crap about me. So I ran into their cell, pushed one against the wall, took his food, and said, "What are you going to do?"

He told the COs, and they put me in the hole for 30 days.

My first 10 minutes out of the hole, a gang member in the pod said, "You owe me money."

"No, I don't," I replied.

"Either pay me or we are fighting," he said.

So I fought him. One of his gang buddies jumped in. It wasn't a brutal fight, but the marks left on each of us garnered attention from the COs, and I went back to the hole.

I eventually had my first court date, and the prosecutor offered me 27 years in prison. I said no and went back to jail, defeated.

I earned enough respect in jail to avoid many more confrontations. I started selling food and drugs to feel like I had some sort of control.

My girlfriend talked to me almost every day, which helped me get through most days. But when I thought about my son and how I let him down, I broke.

After 18 months in jail, I accepted a plea deal for four years with a judicial release after serving six more months in prison, depending on good behavior.

My behavior was anything but good. I found drugs immediately after arriving at Pickaway Correctional Institution and started using them and selling them. Meth and Suboxone were everywhere in the prison.

Prison was not a good place to be high because the walls felt like they were closing in on me. I began hallucinating that my girlfriend was cheating on me with other inmates. My inconsistent behaviors were drawing negative attention, and I found myself fighting regularly.

After taking a brutal beating, I slowed way down on meth. I used Suboxone sparingly due to my fear of becoming addicted and dealing with withdrawals.

A CO found me in possession of Suboxone one day, and I thought my early release was ruined.

Fortunately, the judge had mercy on me, and before too long I was back in county jail preparing for release.

Once released, I went right back to my old ways, using meth. After sitting in guilt for a couple days, I called my probation officer and told on myself. This was the first good decision I had made in a really long time.

I was arrested and taken back to jail. It was at this point that I began making changes.

CHAPTER 19

LEARNING TO STAY

After turning myself in, something inside me started to shift. It wasn't a lightning bolt moment or a big spiritual revelation. It was just a flicker, a sliver of honesty that felt like it could grow.

This time, I started attending a Bible study inside the jail. I didn't fully understand the Scriptures, and truth be told, I wasn't even sure if I believed all of it. But I kept showing up. Week after week, something about the rhythm of sitting in a circle with other broken men reading stories about redemption, forgiveness, and grace started to chip away at the hardness in me.

I also began going to AA meetings.

At first, I hated them. Sitting in a folding chair and listening to people say things like "one day at a time" and "let go and let God" felt cliché and condescending. I didn't want a slogan. I wanted my life back. But then someone said something that stuck.

"You're not weak because you need help. You're strong because you asked for it."

That hit me.

So I kept going.

I was becoming sober—on paper. I wasn't using meth or Suboxone anymore. But emotional sobriety? That was a whole different war. I still had a fuse the length of a matchstick. I still walked around like I had something to prove.

I'd challenge people to fights in group settings. I'd take correction as disrespect. My trauma wore a mask called pride, and I still didn't know how to take it off.

Eventually, I was sent to the Dayton VA Substance Abuse Treatment Program, which felt like a real chance to stabilize. But I wasn't ready for accountability. I was sober, yes, but not surrendered. My body was detoxed, but my spirit was still poisoned by pride, anger, and ego.

I got kicked out.

They told me I wasn't taking the program seriously, that I was a threat to the culture of healing they were trying to create. I argued, cursed, and told them they were weak.

But deep down, I knew they were right.

Getting kicked out of that program was a hard hit, but it was also a mirror. It showed me I hadn't really changed. I was white-knuckling sobriety, but I hadn't lain anything down at the feet of Jesus. I was trying to heal without surrender.

And that never works.

Something had to break—again.

And thank God, it did.

CHAPTER 20

SURRENDER

Getting kicked out of the Dayton VA program was the last straw and the first glimpse of grace.

I had burned through chances, programs, relationships, and reputations. I was sober, but I wasn't healed. I was clean, but I wasn't free. And I was tired—tired of faking it and tired of fighting everything and everyone, including God.

That's when I walked into Southbrook Church and joined the men's group. It was there that someone handed me a book—*Heart of a Warrior* by Michael Thompson.

At first, it felt like just another men's devotional. But as I read deeper, something cracked open inside of me. The book didn't just speak to my behavior; it spoke to my wounds, my past, my father wounds, my shame, and my fear of being known and not being enough.

For the first time, I wasn't just reading a book. The book was reading me.

Through the pages of *Heart of a Warrior*, I began to understand that I wasn't just a screw-up; I was a man with a wounded heart trying to survive. And God wasn't interested in making me behave better. He wanted to heal the places where I was broken. He wanted my heart.

That's when things really started to shift.

I surrounded myself with spiritual leaders—men who were strong and kind, bold and compassionate; men who didn't just hold me accountable but also held space for my story. They were men like Frank Crockett, the Men's Ministry Leader at Southbrook. He saw something in me that I hadn't seen in myself in years—value.

And slowly I began to believe it too.

God started giving me a vision, not just for my own healing but for helping other broken men walk into theirs. I didn't have it all figured out, but I felt called—called into recovery ministry—not because I was perfect but because I was proof that Jesus still raises the dead.

I stayed the course. I showed up. I leaned into community. I finished my probation, something that once felt impossible. And in a beautiful, redemptive twist, I even formed a relationship with Judge Timothy Tepe, the judge who once sentenced me to prison.

Only God.

Then came a divine appointment wrapped in an ordinary day—opening day at a Cincinnati Reds game.

I met a young man there named Jaden. We struck up a conversation, and before the game ended, he invited me to his dad's Saturday morning Bible study. That's where I met his father, Joseph.

Joseph wasn't flashy or loud. He was steady, solid, and present. He lived the gospel more than he spoke it. Alongside David Buckley, another powerful spiritual mentor, Joseph began to disciple me, not just with Scripture but with service. They taught me how to listen, how to be present, and how to take responsibility without shame.

They showed me that true manhood isn't about dominance; it's about discipline, consistency, and compassion. Through their example, I began to realize that God wasn't just calling me out of darkness; He was calling me into leadership.

It was around that same time that I met Steve Ranz, founder of Men Under Construction. Steve quickly became a spiritual mentor. He was sharp in the Word, deep in wisdom, and radically authentic. We began meeting regularly, studying Scripture, and talking about spiritual formation and what it meant to build a life on the rock of Christ.

Eventually, Steve invited me to step deeper into the ministry. That invitation led to me become the cohost of the Men Under Construction podcast, which speaks to men who are tired of pretending and ready to heal. Week after week, we created a space for truth, vulnerability, brotherhood, and biblical identity.

That podcast didn't just help others; it helped me. It became a mirror, a ministry, and a mission.

Week by week, I grew. I was no longer just attending church; I was becoming the Church. I wasn't just studying recovery; I was walking in it. The same streets where I once hustled and numbed out were now the places where I prayed and discipled other men.

God didn't just give me a second chance; He gave me a calling.

And for the first time in my life, I wasn't running away from pain. I was walking others through it.

CHAPTER 21

THE BIRTH OF THE RECOVERY COUCH

I used to think my story disqualified me.

Too many mugshots. Too many felonies. Too many burned bridges, broken hearts, and bent truths. I figured if God wanted to use someone, it'd be the guy with a clean record and a polished life, not a washed-up addict with a prison number and a past full of regret.

But God doesn't call the qualified; He qualifies the called.

And somewhere in the middle of Bible studies, AA meetings, late-night conversations with mentors, and raw moments of quiet honesty, I began to understand that God wanted to use my story—not in spite of it but because of it.

It started as a whisper, an idea I couldn't shake. What if there was a space where people in recovery could be real? What if there was a place where they didn't have to sanitize their testimony or pretend they had it all together? What if there was a place for truth, grace, grit, and the gospel? What if there was a place where you could sit on a metaphorical couch, say the unspeakable, and be met with love, not judgment?

That's how the Recovery Couch was born.

At first, it was just a name, a rough concept. But then I started sharing the vision out loud, and it caught fire. Men and women in recovery, pastors, mentors, and friends didn't just support it; they needed it. I wasn't the only one looking for a place like this.

The more I prayed, the more I felt it in my spirit. God wanted to use my voice, not to glorify my past but to glorify His power, to show others that nothing is wasted. The same God who rescued me from the darkness wanted to shine light through the cracks in my life.

God began calling me into leadership—not the kind that stands on a stage looking down but the kind that sits on the couch beside the broken and says, "Me too. But there's hope."

He showed me that my scars had a purpose. My pain had a platform. My past had prepared me to guide others to freedom. It wasn't about pretending to have all the answers. It was about pointing to the One who does.

Week by week, I started building.

I planned episodes. I wrote outlines. I reached out to people who had walked through hell and lived to talk about it. The guests weren't just clean; they were redeemed. They weren't just sober; they were walking in purpose.

As I sat across from them on that metaphorical couch,

something sacred started to happen. Listeners began to reach out. They heard their own stories in ours. They started to believe that if God could redeem us, then maybe—just maybe—He could redeem them too.

That's when I knew this wasn't just a podcast.

It was a ministry.

It was a movement.

It was a mission from heaven.

And it was personal.

For years, I was the one who needed someone to believe in me, to sit with me, to speak life into the dead parts of my story.

Now I get to be that for someone else.

God had taken my misery and turned it into ministry. He was turning my shame into strength, my pain into purpose, and my testimony into a tool to build His Kingdom.

And I finally understood.

Anything is possible.

CHAPTER 22

FRUIT OF THE COUCH

When I launched the Recovery Couch, I had no idea how far it would go. I didn't have a blueprint. I didn't have a production team or a fancy studio. I had a microphone, a testimony, and a deep conviction that God wanted to use it.

At first, it was slow—a few downloads, a handful of listens. But then people started reaching out.

Not fans. Not followers. Family—brothers and sisters in recovery. People who had never heard the gospel through the lens of addiction. People who were clean but spiritually empty. People who were still using but now had hope.

And they all said something similar: "Thank you for being real. Thank you for telling the truth. Your story helped me believe that I'm not too far gone."

That's when I realized that this was bigger than a podcast. This was God reclaiming territory.

I started hearing from guys in halfway houses and sober

living programs who were streaming episodes on borrowed phones. I heard from wives listening in tears, saying, "My husband's story sounds just like yours." Churches wanted to partner, prisons requested resources, and families held on just a little longer because of a story they heard on the Recovery Couch.

But there was one moment I'll never forget.

It was a young man—I'll call him Marcus. He reached out after hearing an episode where I shared about relapse, guilt, and how I almost gave up after getting out of prison. He said he had just relapsed the night before. His wife had left. His kids didn't want to talk to him. He had one foot in the grave and the other on the gas.

But then at 3:00 a.m., he had put in his earbuds and found the Recovery Couch. He said the only reason he didn't end his life that night was because for the first time, he heard a voice that sounded like his but was filled with hope.

I cried when I read his message, not because of the weight of it but because I knew without a doubt that this was why I went through it all.

God was using my pain to pull someone else back from the edge.

That night was confirmation. The Recovery Couch wasn't just helping people heal, it was keeping people alive. And it was all God.

Since then, the ministry has grown. We've recorded more stories, reached more states, and partnered with more churches. But I've never lost sight of that one listener, that one message, that one soul who needed a reason to hold on.

This is what leadership looks like in the Kingdom. It's not just being the voice behind a mic but being the hands and feet of Jesus behind the scenes—serving, showing up, sharing hope.

God is still writing this story. I'm just grateful He handed me the mic.

CHAPTER 23

FULL CIRCLE

Redemption rarely moves in straight lines. It's more like a divine loop pulling you back to the places where you once fell, not to shame you but to prove that you're no longer the same man who hit the ground.

That's what it felt like the day I stepped back into the prison—not as an inmate but as a speaker.

Same walls. Same gates. Same echo of steel doors slamming shut. But this time, I wasn't wearing orange. I was walking in with a Bible in my hand, purpose in my heart, and freedom in my spirit.

As I stood in front of those men—some just beginning their sentences and others deep in the hopelessness I knew too well—I told my story. Raw. Real. Nothing polished, nothing fake.

I told them about meth and brokenness, about shame and relapse. But I also told them about Jesus, how God didn't just get me out; He came in. Right into the cell. Right into the pit. Right into the mess.

Afterward, one guy walked up slowly, quietly. Then he said, "I want to know God."

We prayed right there, surrounded by concrete and fluorescent lights. And I knew that this is what it was all for.

God was bringing everything full circle, not to haunt me with my past but to use it as a weapon against the enemy. I wasn't just surviving anymore; I was taking ground back.

And it didn't stop there.

As the Recovery Couch grew, so did the vision. God started stretching my imagination, showing me glimpses of what was next. I launched True Story Media, LLC, not just as a business but as a platform to elevate testimonies, fuel recovery efforts, and build bridges between the broken and the redeemed.

Churches, men's groups, prisons, and recovery centers began inviting me to speak. Every stage felt like holy ground.

I was no longer just walking in recovery; I was walking in purpose.

Now I see it clearly. God didn't just rescue me for my own freedom. He called me to set captives free. Through storytelling. Through discipleship. Through the Recovery Couch. Through True Story Media. Through Men Under Construction. Through every mic I'm handed, every man I mentor, and every platform I'm entrusted with.

This isn't about building a brand.

It's about building the Kingdom.

And I know this is just the beginning.

Thank you for being with me on this journey through the highs and the lows, the relapses and the revelations, the prison cells, and the prayer circles. Thank you for giving me the space to tell the truth.

This story isn't just mine. It's a mirror for anyone who's ever felt too far gone. It's for anyone who's ever thought their past disqualified them from purpose. It's for anyone who's ever believed the lie that "this is just the way it'll always be."

I used to believe that too.

I believed I was beyond repair. I believed my mistakes were bigger than God's grace. But I was wrong.

Grace doesn't just cover you; it transforms you. It reaches into the ugliest, most painful places and speaks life. Real life. Eternal life. And it doesn't just save you from your past; it calls you forward into purpose.

I don't have all the answers. I still fall short. I still wrestle with pride and fear and moments of weakness. But I've learned that God isn't looking for perfection. He's looking for surrender. He's looking for men and women who are willing to say, "Here I am. Use me anyway."

This book isn't the end of my story. It's just the beginning of my testimony.

Today, I stand not as a perfect man but as a free one.

Free to love.

Free to lead.

Free to tell the truth.

And if He can do that for me, He can absolutely do it for you.

So wherever you are—whether you're in active addiction, walking through recovery, battling shame, or just quietly wondering if there's more—I want you to hear me clearly.

You're not too far gone.
You're not disqualified.
You're not alone.
God isn't done writing your story.
He's just getting started.

With love,
Brandon Couch

EPILOGUE

If you've made it to this page, thank you—not just for reading my story but for feeling the weight of it. Thank you for honoring the messy middle, the heartbreak, the hard truths, and the hope that somehow still rises.

I didn't write this book to be a hero. I wrote it because I survived, and survival comes with responsibility to tell the truth. To shine a light. To remind someone else that they're not too far gone. That failure isn't final. That God still shows up in the darkest places.

Healing didn't come all at once. It came in pieces through accountability. Through prayer. Through relapses and restarts. Through community and calling. Through grace—undeserved but freely given.

If you're holding this book and still wrestling with your own Step 4, take your time. Be honest. Be brave. And above all, believe this: There's purpose in your pain, and there's hope on the other side.

And when you're ready, your story can set someone else free too.

The journey isn't easy, but it's worth every step.

A NOTE TO MY CHILDREN

To my son and daughter,

You didn't get to choose the parts of my story that touched your lives, but I pray this book helps you understand the man I was, the man I've become, and the man I fight every day to be. You are my greatest reason for choosing recovery, over and over again. I hope one day you'll read these pages and see not just the pain but the purpose. I hope you'll know that redemption is real and that no matter where life takes you, you are never too far from grace.

I love you more than words could ever tell.

—Dad

NEXT STEPS AND RESOURCES

If you're ready to begin your own recovery journey or support someone you love—here are some trusted resources to help you take the next step.

12-Step and Faith-Based Programs:

Celebrate Recovery: www.celebraterecovery.com
Alcoholics Anonymous: www.aa.org
Narcotics Anonymous: www.na.org
Regeneration Recovery: www.regenerationrecovery.org

Mental Health and Counseling:

Psychology Today Therapist Finder: www.psychologytoday.com
Faithful Counseling: www.faithfulcounseling.com
SAMHSA's National Helpline (Free and Confidential): 1-800-662-HELP (4357)

Stay Connected:
>The Recovery Couch Podcast
>YouTube: @RecoveryCouch
>Website: www.recoverycouch.com
>Instagram: @recoverycouch

You are not alone.
There is help. There is healing. There is hope.

www.ingramcontent.com/pod-product-compliance
Lightning Source LLC
Chambersburg PA
CBHW062115080426
42734CB00012B/2874